Ecstatic Soul

" Feel the connection "

fuzail khan

ISBN 978-93-5458-593-7
© fuzail khan 2021
Published in India 2021 by Pencil

A brand of
One Point Six Technologies Pvt. Ltd.
123, Building J2, Shram Seva Premises,
Wadala Truck Terminal, Wadala (E)
Mumbai 400037, Maharashtra, INDIA
E connect@thepencilapp.com
W www.thepencilapp.com

Author biography

Fuzail Khan is the new indie author. he is currently a student at Jamia Millia Islamia. this book is the first-ever book written by him at the age of 17.

CONTENTS

Part 1

Eternal Endurance

From the darkest hours of one's life, the most beautiful moment is something which is called patience. When the wind tickled the trees when the mountains presented the grief of being still and the birds sobbed for their loved ones.

There was a dwelling in between a valley. In that house breathed an old man. He was painting something, something very special. His sallow, wrinkled face recounts a story. The story of longing for someone. The river alongside was describing a tale that faded in the pages of his life.

We sometimes misremember some events, but some events got clasped in mind like our fate.

The sun wanted to leave him, and the only thing left in his life was darkness. He left his chair and took his basket. He was so pale that he took his stick with him and went outside. Furthermore, he steps gently and calmly. He went through the dark forest, the birds were on his shoulders, with the memory of his love, he saw those little rabbits, with which his devotion played. **He took those rabbits on his lap and looked into their eyes as if he was looking in his own heart. Likewise, he tries to find him, but he finds nothing.**

It is difficult to find someone in your soul who has already escaped. You try your best to find the one, but he disappeared, and the only thing left is pain. It is the love that makes your soul warm, without it, you are alone.

The old man walked ahead in the forest, at the river he relaxed for a while, he put his basket aside and observed the fishes. He recalled the old days when he was fishing with his son. he gave the bigger fish to his son. He abruptly smiles and the downpour from his eyes drops down gently. With an exhalation, he took his basket and moved ahead.

Remembering old fantasies makes us nostalgic and remembering them more and more makes us flawed. Walk every day solely, do every task without the help of anyone. sleep when the birds sleep and wake up when the sun wakes. such was the life of that old man " a feeling of aloofness".

Ahead on the hills, he went to a place where he hardly goes, his old hut.

The hut was dusty and dull. Many birds and animals were there as if they were having a celebration there or maybe the old man was one of the inmates.

The animals bowed in his respect, and the birds were circling above him. He walked like an old ruler with finesse. Inside his old house, he found his old essence. Below his bed, he found some trinkets and paintings of his son. little t-shirts, little pants and some toys. He scented them and took some paintings with him.

Those paintings tell him the tale of his son's childhood. When he was at the age of 3, he didn't know how to walk. His mother and father taught him how to step. He took three weeks to walk on his feet, and at that time his father sketched this landscape. At the age of 15 when he obliged a book, his father went to a nearby settlement to buy it. Teaching the first word to a child needs tonnes of hard work and sanctification.

Then he went to the backyard of his hut and he took the shovel. He saw that the yard's grass had grown so much, so he cut them as well. When he finished that task, he went towards the forests with all the birds and animals. He rested in some spots because he was so weak. He plucked some fresh fruits and gave some to the animals. With slow steps and running breath, he walked towards a place where it was so dark.

He had some fruits and some flowers whose fragrance was clinching him, the presence of someone. He smiled and gave those flowers to her. He shares some fruits with her as well. He talked about his visit to their old house and their child's toys and paintings. **"It is hard to forget someone close to one's heart. Sooner or later one will have to separate."** Because separation is the root of a reunion. Love is eternal and so is the union.

"You are close to my heart and soul, whether you are beneath the soil, and I am on the ground. Every day, the old man came to his wife's grave to talk to her and eat with her. On each day there was a reunion of love and soul." But the old man had to leave because he could not delay his work.

The old man asked for her regards and left. The sun returned from his home, and so was the old man.

No sleep, no hunger for breakfast, the longing of his loved one was enough for him. He started to dig the ground and went into his house. Put his basket aside and sat on his chair and started painting again. Wherever his paint drained, his tears added some wetness to it.

Life gives us a lot, but we don't thank it. When it has some dry spells, we have to make it wetter by love. In the dry spells of the old man's life, he was trying to make it wetter by his tears. "His tears were his love and that painting was his life".

Part 2

Beginning's End

In the days of spring, when there was peace throughout, there was his first call, a first cheer. On that day, a cute, wonderful baby was born. Leaving his mother and father remarkably pleasant. They named him "Zen". His face was like a new blooming flower and his body was as shimmering as the sun. His mother was very happy on that day, but her condition was not good. Gem's father brought a doctor from the nearby village. The doctor gave her some medicine and advised her to rest for a few days.

On that occasion, the zen's father made a swing, which he will give him on his 3rd birthday. The kind of feeling that Gem's father was having can be felt by any parent. If I talk about soul and love from the perspective of a parent, then a child is the only soul and love for his/her parents. On his 3rd birthday, his father gave him that hand made swing. But he refused to accept that because he wanted a new toy just like any other child in the village. At that age, he went to the village school, which was around 6 km away. His father took him to school and took him back from there. He was turning into a stubborn child. He always wants expensive stuff. His parents gave it to him.

At night, his mother tells him stories and teaches him lessons from them. One day his mother told him a story of a man who lives in the forests. He was alone, and he lived his life in the darkness of the forest with animals and birds. He became so weak and sick that one day he died and the animals and birds dug his grave and buried him underneath the earth. The child questioned, why the old man was alone and how he survived alone in that forest. His mother answered that **"everybody in this world is alone, but there was one thing that kept him alive, and that was the connection of his soul with his love. He was waiting for his love, but his love was not there, therefore his soul was waiting for his love".**The child said: "but you told me that he was dead ". Mother answered: *only his body became dead, not his soul. The soul is immortal, it cannot die. It is still there waiting for his love.*

Mother said it right, the soul is immortal. Humans are troubled kind, they don't know what true love is. Only a soul knows what real love is. and that's the case with the man in that story. Stories correlate to us in our lives. Some stories are inspirational, some are fantasy and some are real aspects of one's life. **"Our life is a story, and it isn't so long. We are the authors of our stories, and the ending of these stories is death. But the soul doesn't fit in these diminutive stories, instead, its real story is the voyage of finding true love and death may be embarkation for it but not the end".**

The boy was grown up and it was a moment for him to go to college. His father travelled with him to a college for admission in a town located far away from the valley. He was admitted into that college. he had to live there because the college was too far from his residence. His father understands the circumstances, but the longing of his son was intolerable for his mother. She was weeping when he was leaving. He was going as he would never come.

It is hard to live without your loved ones, but each one has to live their own life and each one has to die one day. His father began painting, which he left many years ago. He paints day and night. He painted every moment of his son's life. *"The brushes were never dried, the paint was never left in the buckets. The time from his life was given to the papers. His blood was flowing on the paper and the paper was absorbing his blood for his blood (his son)"*. "The story does not end yet, it is the beginning of the end".

Part 3

Exceptional Essence

Zen, on his first day of college, was very nervous and feeling homesick. He was living in a shared room with his flatmates. One of his roommates, Danny, had a very good soul. He lived in that house for about 2 years and knew everything regarding the town and college. He helped a Zen to settle down in that town.

From a valley to a town, this drastic change is very diverting for the gem, and he felt very nervous in that city. On the first day of his college, he was very nervous, not for his study but for making friends. He was so handsome that every girl wanted to be his fellow but he was so careful in this.

We all want a friend like us. A person who has all those feelings like us. We always make those friends who like our personality or our moods, but sometimes we acquire some bad habits from them."In this world the only friend you have is time. Time teaches us what is right and what is wrong. But when it leaves us, we are left with nothing.

This life (inevitable to time) has some phases. Our **first phase**is our childhood, where time welcomes us into this world, time knows that we are the new chapters of this life so it won't be harsh on us. For some 10-12 years it plays with us like a child, becoming happy when we are happy, becoming sad when we are sad. Then it moves with us into the **second phase,**our teenage life. In this phase, time builds our creativity and curiosity. time knows that the third phase would be difficult for the person, so it gives us teaching from an early stage, some take the teaching while some do not. Then comes the most important phases of time where time starts to become harsh, and that phase is called the **young life phase**. This phase is most difficult to pass as there are a lot of difficulties and distractions given by time.

This phase contains a sub-phase, which is the sweetest phase of all and that phase is called **love**. This phase generally gives a feeling of compassion and caring for the other soulmate. But sometimes we don't have those inclinations to perceive what is good for ourselves and what is bad. And in this confusion, we lost both.

while for Zen, that is not the case, he found his true love, but in which phase of time he doesn't know. In his final year of college, when he was doing his task in the library. A gorgeous girl sat beside him. When Zen looked towards her he was totally lost in her eyes, he kept looking into her eyes, there was no such satisfactory matter for him as looking into her eyes. He became lost in them. In his heart was only a picture of her. Simultaneously the girl has also fallen in love.

The most beautiful moment in someone's life is the first feeling of love, a feeling of tranquillity. Both of them also felt the same. ***"but they don't know that there is one more feeling which is more intense than this"***. The next day, they both met in the library and this time, Zen asked her name, she said her name was Jessica. They both became friends. That night Zen told the whole synopsis to his roommate Danny. Danny told him that Jessica was a rich man's daughter and she would not be ready to marry him. But Zen was blind in her love and wanted to try his luck even if she belonged to a well-to-do family.

On Thursday evening, both met in the cafe. Both were as silent as figures. Then Jessica said that she loved him and wanted to marry him. But Zen said that he is broke. Surprisingly, she accepted his condition and said that both will move into a big city after marriage and live in her father's house. Without a second thought, he accepted her condition. He doesn't even think about his parents. Danny once again warned him that this decision will be bad for him and his parents, but he didn't take that seriously. He doesn't know what his parents' condition was.

Part 4

Last Breath

Several years passed. The man and woman became old and weak. Gem's mother was very ill and weak, she was on the bed and her time was closed. The only thing she wanted to see was her child's face. But she didn't know that his child would never come.

Her husband always convinced her to go to the hospital with him in a nearby village. But she denied it every time. The old man went to the town to see his son but he found no one. The old man didn't say anything to his wife because he knows that she will not be able to suffer from that news.

On the other hand, his son was savouring life with his wife after marriage. He was living in a palace-like house with a lot of helpers. He now runs a company with his wife and was the proprietor of half of her property. This is all because her wife loves him so much.

How bad is that person who has everything but does not have loved ones? And how good is that person who doesn't have anything but the love of loved ones. a person always wants everything in his life but he doesn't praise those things which were granted to him. On the bed of death, Zen's mother was laid and the countdown of her separation was started. Her husband was beside her telling her some stories of the past just like she tells the stories to her son. **When you are old, you become a child, you need someone just as you were to take care of your child. And the only one you need is your child if he/she is not there then, how hard is it for those who need you**.

Taking her last breath she said to her husband that she wanted him to communicate a letter to her child. The words were of her but the writing was of her husband. Her letter is written below:

Dear son,

"God give me only a few breaths to talk to you. I know that you are so busy with your work and you have no time to come here. And when you come here, you will only see my grave and flowers on it. Don't think that I will not wait for you, you know that once upon a time I told you a story in which I tell you that only the body dies not the soul, the soul is immortal and it will live forever. Just like that, my soul will wait for you and I know that one day you will come and live with your father. I know that you are a good person and you will not hurt your parents, one day you will come and see me. Look, son, the real pleasure in life is death, and don't you worry about me, I am going to enjoy that pleasure. but my peace lies in you. If you are in trouble I will be in trouble too. Now, I am leaving, leaving this world but not from you. Love you…Your mother".

With this last word, she left this world. Her husband doesn't cry, instead, he smiles and looks at her because he knows that she is still close to him, somewhere in his heart.

When your close ones leave you, there is a deep sense of sadness in you. But I think that one day we will meet them and until then we need to be patient. And let me tell you that, patience is real love. When your face smiles and your heart cries… that is patience. When you try to be happy and your heart is in constant sadness, that is patient. Love is patience and this love is connected with your soul, you just have to feel that connection.

The old man buried his wife in the middle of the forest and spent some nights there. Without food, he became weak but he didn't feel hungry. He took some logs and axes and went alongside the river to build a new cottage for himself. It took 2 weeks to complete the building of his new cottage. He wanted a small space where he could spend his last years in peace.

The sound of the river flows, birds' chirping, and the open sky helped him be closer to nature. The land was his rug and the sky was his tent and he was resting in a house which he had to leave one day. The more you try to fit in this world, the more you will be lost. This world is best for those who treat it as an inn.

The one who wants to reside in it forever will not find even a single spot. The fate of mankind is life and death and he has to accept it. just as the old man was.

Part 5

Lost Path

Zen was now a successful businessman. He divorced his wife because they don't have good mutual harmony. He is now into criminal activity. Some people say - 'To be a wealthy person you need some sort of black money and Zen was in that as well. His thinking had now changed and his brain had concealed the memories of his parents. Money is something that makes a person deaf, dumb and blind. He was also enjoying his luxurious life because he knew that if a person has money, he doesn't need love, nor does he need those people who loved him. Money becomes his desire and his love.

There is a constant battle between the heart and the brain. The brain doesn't know the feeling but the heart knows. The heart knows which is right for you and which is wrong. But if the brain tricks you and gets full control of yourself, then, in that case, your heart gets locked. And when your heart is locked, your soul will not return to you, then you have no inner feeling or emotion. The same was happening with Zen, he didn't know that his heart and soul were locked somewhere inside him.

The old man, on the other hand, had grown very old. He barely heard and his sight was also very weak. His whole day was spent painting and writing letters to his son. He wrote many letters and posted them in the town where his son once studied. One of his letters is written beneath:

To zen, " How are you, my son? This is my 150th letter. And it's been 8 years since your mother passed away. But you haven't replied to any of my letters. I don't know where you are but I know that you don't forget us. I know you are busy, but don't you have some time to reply to my letter? I am turning old with each passing day, my body doesn't support me and surely that day is near when death finds me and takes me away. I don't afraid of death, all I want is to see your face before closing my eyes. I know that in your childhood, I didn't give you what you wanted but don't give me such pain which I can't endure. This letter is the last letter from me and if you receive this letter, come as fast as you can, try not too late because death is punctual in its tasks".Your father...

How hard it is to sustain the endeavour of your love, especially if you have a blood relation. The eternal pain is for those who wait for their loved ones. But someone who doesn't see anything before money, love is not the priority, love is not the responsibility, love is not endurance, love is nothing but a sensation that he lost somewhere in his inner self.

A man has two paths, one is right and the other is wrong. The one who chooses the wrong path must have a chance to turn back to the right. God gives everyone a chance of being good, but sometimes you need to pay back the blood money of your bad deeds. Even life became a web of spiders in which his humanity got trapped and he had only one way to get out of that and that was to destroy himself, to destroy his personality.

He has to kill himself, destroy his personality and make a new one. A man can change his personality but he cannot change his desires. "Desires only need an end".And if you fail to change your desire, then desires will end you. Killing the desires is not easy, desire is a fire inside your heart. And the only thing which can kill this fire is the fire itself. A fire of positivity, a fire of love.

Maybe Jessica's love was not true love, that's why both got separated. Love doesn't always mean a woman, it can be anything, anything which gives you comfort, peace in your heart. Zen had a bigger struggle to find his true love. Maybe he was not lost. Yet he was late but will surely find a correct way, sooner or later. Zen's father, searching for someone day and night.

No. it was not Zen but someone who gave him peace of heart and soul. He wanders days and nights over the hills. In search of his tranquillity, in search of someone, who was greater than the sky, and vast as land, and closer to him than his heart. His voyage had now started, the connection was going to be built…

Part 6

Ecstasy of Nature

On the mountain, he was seeking someone. While walking he found a cave. He took sanctuary there for some time. He was constantly thinking about divine power. His mind wasn't aware of such a power that causes downpour, who had fixed the time of sun, moon, and stars in the sky, who knows every secret of mortality and creation.

He went to the mountains and asked them, ***"Oh, mountains, don't you know who is your creator, who nurtured you, made you higher... don't you know who is your lord..."*** still like always, there was no reply, not a word. This silence answered all his questions. Mountains didn't know who their creator was. The man got downhearted and moved onward. While he was going, out of the blue, heavy rainfall started, resisting him to go forward. He took shelter around the shed and started to roar again. ***"Oh, heavy downpour, how a huge cloud may pour little drops, who created you, who replenishes water in your grimy nature". With a wail, he said, " don't you know who your lord is?" I want to meet him. Can you tell me where he lives? I wanted to tell him that there is nobody with me, I am alone, my cherished ones left me. I will tell him that my road is evacuated and I don't know where my end is. And now, I only want to meet you...I only yearn to meet you..."***

At night he was in the cave. Looking at the sky from the corner of the cave. His eyes were shimmering like a star in the sky. There was gloom everywhere. He was looking for divine power for one month. He asked everyone about it but nobody knew. Everybody was just doing their tasks and no one complained.

The old man's childhood was spent in forests and he didn't know about that divine power "GOD". His parents passed away when he was 8 years old. From then on he became an atheist and lived the rest of his life being like that. His wife and son were also atheists. Maybe he had some belief but who knows.

When he woke up the next morning, he saw a bird feeding her babies. Animals near the lakes were bathing. When he saw these situations, he felt light in his heart, he suddenly became very cherished. He called some birds by a whistle and played with them for a little while. Within a month he became the friend of every animal and bird. Now, he is back home again. He was becoming friendly to every being of nature. He had a love for all those beings in his heart. Now his soul felt the calmness of love. But there is no treatment for the love of the exalted one. It's been nine years and his child was not there with him. This pain turns his ecstasy into misery, his ease into grief.

Part 7

Dwelling Chest

It was time for him to take that out. he knew that he could find all the answers in that box. Somewhere, around a distance of 3 miles from the river, it was buried. The box was given to him by his grandfather. He told him not to open it until he needed it. Throughout his life, he never felt the need for that box. But now it was time for him to open it.

He took his shovel and went out in search of that box. He knew that he would find the box but never thought about what was inside it. Maybe old clothes from his childhood or maybe some money but what was the need for money and childhood memories in the old man's life. Maybe the secret of his identity was hidden inside that box.

A new journey towards the forests near the hills, he doesn't know what was inside that box, but he knows that his grandfather had put some best things inside that box. The hope of identity, the hope of the divine makes his feet move forward. Somewhere around the hill, he started digging the ground, but he found nothing… nothing there. He moves ahead. In the middle of the forest, there were flower blossoms for the old man as if they were welcoming the successor of identity. He remembers that in his childhood, he visited that place with his grandfather and his grandfather picked some roses from there for his grandmother. and one day both came there again to bury the box. "the chest of mystery".

He started digging there. And with a seventh strike, he found something rigid... Yes, that was the box. With a shiny appearance, the box was still shining like a star even after 40 years. On that box there was something written, something like that: "feel the connection, so that you can live eternally. Only death is your break, but your life goes on." After reading those phrases, the old man's whole body shivers. In his ears, echoes the words of his wife: " only the body dies not the soul, the soul is immortal and it will live forever."

He took that chest with him and moved forward to his address. While walking, he continuously thinks about his grandfather. He felt a longing for his childhood. When he was a child, he used to play with his grandmother. He saw her as his mother and roamed around here and there with her but after her death he became alone, no one was with him not even his grandparents.

Now he is a parent, he also doesn't have his child with him. Life's games are different, whether you win in this game or lose, or the game is over and you don't even know. He knew where the key was. He opened his old drawer and he found it. He unlocked the box and opened it. What he found was nothing but papers and papers...something was drawn on those papers.

The old man was unaware of that type of language. But there was a letter in that box as well. When the old man saw that letter he started reading it. It took about 3-4 hours to understand it or you can say to believe in it. The tears knew where to flow and they were doing what they knew. He could not control his emotions and started crying. He cried for many hours.

he didn't know where to stop. Maybe, one can understand his feeling if he or she could have found that his whole life was nothing, and the period in which he called "a life" was just a dream, a dream in which nothing would benefit him. Neither his loved ones nor his identity. The letter was written by his late father who died early before his birth.

"This letter will go to my child, Ahmad." I know we hide this secret with you. But it is not something that can be shared easily. We are from the lineage of an Arabic calligrapher. For centuries we have been painting the attributes and blessings which are given to us by our God 'the almighty'. But I and your grandfather could not do so because this duty not only needs the capability of one's hand but also needs the connection between you and the almighty God. We tried very hard but couldn't do it. I think that you will have that connection by birth, I wanted to teach but my time span is now going to be over. When you find this box, you will become capable of doing this task. I know that you will do it and your descendants too…"

He took one sheet and tried to understand it. But it was an unknown script for him. He suddenly took his stick and went to his old house. he knew that his wife loved to read books and he surely knew that there was a book to understand that language. It was a new life for the old man. Ahmad found his new soul, this name gave him the peace and the identity he was finding.

Perhaps Ahmad has that spiritual connection. That is why he endured so much pain after his child left him. Life was not as straight as the road on which Ahmad was going. zen's life was also not like that, filled with a lot of twists. you got mystified in this twisted life, but one day you found the right path.

35

Part 8

Locked Heart

The heart feels it first. The sorrows of life, the happiness of still living, the faces of people and the love given by them. All these feelings are felt by only the heart," the heart feels it first". But what if someone's heart is locked? All these feelings are then concealed within one's heart. The mind doesn't see good or bad, nor does it see the punishment of doing bad.

That is what Zen is doing in his life. He ran his business in a bad manner and couldn't try to understand the theory of the good. But one day he realised that the work he was doing was just a dream, a dream of lunacy. He had been put behind bars for doing illegal activities. He was put in jail, breathed by some like-minded people. He was put in with an old man of around 55. His name was Qadeer.

When Zen entered the jail, Qadeer was praying to his lord. He wore a white sheet on his head and was weeping constantly. Zen thought that he was weeping because of the punishment that was given by the in-charge. Zen sat in a corner and started observing him. The next day, around five Qadeer again sat in that posture and started crying. When Zen woke up he saw the same scenario again. This time he asked him: "Why are you crying". Did you make some mistakes?

He answered: "every person in this world commits some mistake, but the better one is he who repents for it". But repent to whom? Do you have anyone who is bigger than you"?"Time gives the answers... no one can find their answer without the permission of time. But time is also someone's slave, the slave of my God." Qadeer words were playing with Zen.

he asked Zen why he was in jail. Then, Zen told him that he was messed up in illegal activities. Qadeer said: "Maybe you will one day get out of jail but how will you survive in this world while your identity is locked."In this world, we have two identities. One which is apparent to people and one which is inside us.

People know our outer identity but they are unaware of our inner identity and so are we. We sometimes aren't able to see our inner identity, but if someday we realize it then it is the best day to visualize it. That day was of the old man, he was in his old home searching for the book he wanted because he wanted to visualize his identity.

He finally found the book. Its name was "for calligraphy". He opened that book and on the initial page it was written: "for those who deserve it". Simultaneously he thought about whether he deserves it or not. Then he remembered his father's letter and started reading it. That book taught me how to do calligraphy and its history and its significance. Ahmad started practising it. It took him around 5-6 months to master it. Now he knew who he was and he started praying to his lord.

He knew that one day his child would come and he would then tell him his true identity and pass that skill to him.

But this thing is even harder than learning calligraphy. The first piece of calligraphy he made was of the attribution of his Lord called "Rehman". He was understanding the connection of his soul with calligraphy. But this connection was still imperfect because the main aspect which needed it was its existence. The old man didn't have infinite years to live.

Qadeer sat beside Zen and asked him what his religion was. He replied that he had no religion nor did he worship any God. Qadeer asked once again what his religion was, he said that he had no religion. Qadeer said, "do you love anyone?" He said yes I loved the girl who used to be my wife but we divorced. "Do you love any other being?" said Qadeer. Zen contemplated his mind and suddenly, with no expression, he said: "my parents", with this a drop of his sorrow came out from his eyes. Qadeer asked - " where are they?" In my heart", he replied. Qadeer smiled and said: "your heart is locked, you have to open it so that you can see where your parents are". "I know where they are but don't know whether they are living or dead." "It's been 15 years since I left my home and now if I go…" he stopped there and started crying."You have to know what your mission on this earth is, if you cry for nothing, it will not help you," Qadeer said loudly.

Qadeer then went to the room's corner and took his sacred religion book (Quran). He recited a verse from it then told its meaning. He said: 'Every person in this world has a mission, when the correct time comes, every human knows what he has to do. Suddenly, a sound crackled inside his body. It was like something was constantly being broken. Maybe it was the chains that were bound to his heart. The sacred book was healing his soul and heart. He was feeling the love for his parents.

With each passing day, he was understanding and learning the lessons from Quran from Qadeer. The message he was getting from it was breaking the chains of his heart. It was like his soul was hungry for the past 15 years and now it is getting its food.

 But the time span for each human is fixed in this world. Zen also knows that he doesn't have much time to meet his parents. Maybe one of them was dead or both… this thought came to mind every night when he slept. That was the toughest time of his life. But when someone finds peace in his life, his life becomes like an old man. He knew what was doing and what God chose for him

Part 9

Only Feeling

"He was painting something, something very special. His sallow, wrinkled face tells a story. The story of longing for something or someone. The river alongside his house was telling a story that had faded in the pages of his life". We sometimes misremember some events, but some events got clasped in mind like our fate.

These lines are taken from the first chapter of this book. It is because now is the right time to talk about it. We have seen the journey of Zen and Ahamd and seen how fate has changed their lives. But the story is not complete yet.

One day Zen felt something inside his heart as if his heart had been unlocked. Zen closed his eyes and started contemplating. When he closed his eyes, his heart opened, he could see the mountains, birds, animals, blue sky and an old person. His face was not clear but when he saw a ring on his hand. He realised that he was his father. Like the crystal of the ring, his eyes dropped a crystal of remembrance, he started crying and cried for an hour.

Qadeer was watching him and he knew that Zen's heart had changed and now he can choose his destiny or maybe destiny had already chosen him. after these sorrowful days and nights, one day he finally said to Qadeer that he wanted to accept his religion (Islam). Qadeer asked him whether he wanted to accept it of his own will or not? Zen said that he wanted to accept it of his own will.Qadeer recites (kalmah), some special sentences to accept Islam and Zen repeated those sentences.

Zen didn't know that the sentence which was repeating was in his blood since his birth. He accepted it. Now he knew his identity, but he could not go to his home as he was not released yet. He had to spend around 3 years in jail. After 2 years in jail, Zen became a religious and pious person. Qadeer on the other hand, became ill with some disease and had a fever. The doctor did some treatment but medicines did not affect him. On his last day, Qadeer called Zen close and had a chat with him.

His last words were like that: **"I have been put into this jail for no reason. It has now been 15 years since I have been here in front of you. Maybe my punishment will increase, so it is better that I die because it gives me a better place to live. Keep one thing in your heart that this world is a jail for us. Whichever path we choose, we have to face punishments and difficulties, but in the end, what you find is freedom. If we choose the right path and our destination will be good and if we choose the wrong path then our destination will be grim. I am going but my soul is with you. I like your company and one last request: don't forget me and the teaching which I gave you because mankind dies, but their teaching remains...remains..."**

With these words, he goes into a deep sleep. Going into that good deep sleep. We have to be awake for our whole life, when we are awakened only then we will accurately use our mind and listen to our heart. Someone good like Qadeer came into our problematic life and became a source of our change. People like Qadeer are the best people in this world. Their motive to give people the right path makes them worthy of paradise.

There are some people in this world who sacrifice their lives for their loved ones. Love is something that makes them happy from the outside but rusty from the inside. The expression of love is something that feels in the heart and tickles you throughout your life. When your loved one left you … it is something which cannot be explained. And when they suddenly come in front of you, the wound deep inside your heart becomes fresh again and suddenly you feel the pain but you cannot express it. That is the feeling of being loved. Some emotions are dead but love is something that lives when you die in yourself, you are like a dead robot, you can walk, talk and do any sort of work but you cannot express your emotion. Like a dead scarecrow, Ahmad also wanted to express his love but no one shared his love.

His wife was beneath the earth. And his son left him. He had only one thing and that was his connection. That connection was healing his soul and giving him the patience to endure pain for his love. ***"He smiled and gave those flowers to her. He shares some fruits with her as well. He talked about his visit to their old house and their child's toys and paintings. It is hard to forget someone close to one's heart. Sooner or later*** *we will have to separate. Because separation is the key to a reunion. Love is eternal and so is the union. You are close to my heart and soul, whether you are beneath the soil, and I am on the ground. Every day, the old man came to his wife's grave to talk to her and eat with her. On each day there was a reunion of love and soul." (from chapter 1)*

He was growing weak and ill but he was constantly writing and making calligraphy. He was also digging something. He took his father's ring and his grandfather's letters and put them in the box. On top of that, he pasted Zen's mother's first and last letter.

He took that box with him and put it near the digging area. Suddenly he fainted and fell to the ground. No one could help him and sprinkle some water on him. But who needs a person when there is the Almighty with one's. After some time the cloud saw the old man and sprinkled some water on him. Somehow his eyes opened and he pushed himself toward the house. But he didn't want to rest, he wanted to complete his last calligraphy painting. He knows that his time to meet his lord is close. But he wanted to see his son before he died.

Every story has an ending because every story is based upon humans and every human has an ending. I hope its last chapter doesn't end the story because each story gives us a message and we have to use those messages in our story...story of life.

45

Part 10

Meeting place

 when he was contemplating his lord. Suddenly the jailor came. He would have seen him for 5 years and had seen a change in him and his behaviour. With a heavy voice, he said," your time here is over". Zen suddenly looked at him and said, "but I have to spend 2 more years. Jailor said, " one of your friends has applied for bail and now it is accepted, you are free now." "but … who, I don't know any of my friends". Zen said. "Come out first...I will take you there".

When Zen saw him, he couldn't remember him because in front of him there was a man who had a thick beard and he was looking like a saint. " I am your friend Danny but now my name is qalb." Zen couldn't understand what was going on there, after a while he understood that Danny was his roommate from college time. He was an entirely different person than before. What made him like that? That question was running in Zen's mind like a running horse.

Then Qalb said, " your father…". what? What about my father? Where is he? After listening to what Qalb had said to him, he ran as if he would never stop. What did Qalb tell him? But it was something very important to Zen, that is why he rams in that way."After you left that city with Jessica, I started getting letters from your father. I thought they were worried about you, but when I saw a letter each week , I realised that something is very important which your father wants to tell, so once I opened a letter from your father and read it. When I read it...I completely got into it and then I couldn't stop myself from reading those letters. I have been searching for you for 10 years but I couldn't find you. I am now a muslim and that's because of those letters. ***Those words have made me their slave and I didn't want to release from that salavery***. That is why I accepted your religion… your legacy is calling you...he had no time… go there as fast as you can

." That's where he stopped talking and ran to his father. Some words can change the life of a human but some words are there which can change the soul. Danny, who is now Qalb, found his new heart and soul. The meaning of his name also gives the testimony of that.For some people, the meeting place is somewhere in the world. But some meetings are held in the deepest corner of your heart where no one except you can find you.

"Remembering old memories makes us nostalgic and remembering them more and more makes us imperfect. Walk every day solely, do every task without the help of anyone. sleep when the birds sleep and wake up when the sun wakes. that was the life of that old man " a feeling of aloofness".

This phrase shows the old man's feelings in the first chapter but now it is best suited to his son. The desire which he wants is nothing now. All he wants is his father, the one who loved him the most. At that point, he knew that his mother was dead. Slowly and gradually he was losing everything. Each step he took, walking towards his destiny, the destiny which will give him satisfaction and peace. The old man was completing his last calligraphy. Zen and the angel of death, both were coming. But we don't know who was faster? His life or his fate?

Epilogue

Meeting Place

He reached his destination. He moved his leg slowly. The silence welcomed him in the dark forest, the mountains were mourning and the birds and animals were attending his last day in this world. With a bawl, he spoke "baba". He was crying loudly. With his cry birds and animals ran away. When he reached towards the grave. He saw an engraving on his father's grave, on it was written "Ahmad, the patient one". He didn't know who wrote it but he realised that his father's name was Ahmad.

Then he went to his house and found a pile of calligraphy hanging on the wall. He picked the last one which was on the table. He wasn't able to understand it. Then he went out and sat near his father's grave. He put the last calligraphy on his father's grave. Then he saw the box on which his mother's last letter was. He read it and cried for hours and hours. He was crying because he was not there in the harshest times of his parents' life.

Later he opened the box and started to understand the stuff in it. But he was not in a situation where he could understand anything. This was his last day in this world because he lost the one who made him alive. Although he had his God. he controlled himself and went to his mother's grave as well. Back at his father's grave, he had that box and the last calligraphy of his father.

The main thrust which one has to quench is his life and his death. Zen had both of them, he wanted to live his life like his father with the help of that box and the second thing which he had was his father's last painting, which was a message for him. Zen wasn't able to translate that word, but it was something which his father knew and that was "Azal", which means death.

He knows that, when you have the love of your lord, all you need to live with him and one has to cross a path of death in order to reach his lord.

"From the darkest hours of one's life, the most beautiful moment is something which is called patience. When the wind tickled the trees and the mountains presented the grief of being still, the birds sobbed for their loved ones." not only birds, but even humans sobbed for their loved ones. Now he had to be patient to meet his parents.

Night covered the sky and it was cold all around. Zen was sleeping, putting his head on his father's grave. two souls came and sat beside him, one put a cloth on him so he wouldn't feel the cold and the other one titillated his hand on his head.

www.ingramcontent.com/pod-product-compliance
Lightning Source LLC
LaVergne TN
LVHW050425160726
843469LV00041B/1228